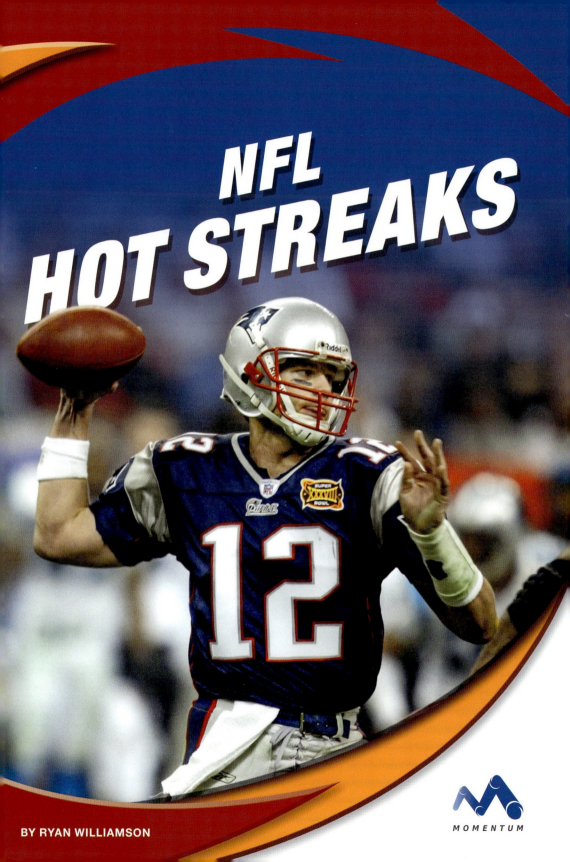

NFL HOT STREAKS

BY RYAN WILLIAMSON

Published by The Child's World®
1980 Lookout Drive • Mankato, MN 56003-1705
800-599-READ • www.childsworld.com

Photographs ©: Tom DiPace/AP Images, cover, 1, 18; Action Sports Photography/Shutterstock Images, 5; NFL Photos/AP Images, 6; AP Images, 8, 9; Bill Sikes/AP Images, 10; Al Messerschmidt Archive/AP Images, 12; Red Line Editorial, 13; Al Golub/AP Images, 14; Paul Sakuma/AP Images, 17; Hans Deryk/AP Images, 21; Tom DiPace/AP Images, 22; Jim Rogash/AP Images, 24; Tom Olmscheid/AP Images, 26; Jim Mone/AP Images, 28

Copyright © 2020 by The Child's World®
All rights reserved. No part of this book may be reproduced or utilized in any form or by any means without written permission from the publisher.

ISBN 9781503832282
LCCN 2018963089

Printed in the United States of America
PA02422

ABOUT THE AUTHOR

Ryan Williamson is a sportswriter based in the Minneapolis–Saint Paul, Minnesota, area. He has written articles that have appeared in various publications across the country. He graduated from the University of Missouri with a degree in print/digital sports journalism.

CONTENTS

FAST FACTS 4

CHAPTER ONE
The Perfect Season 7

CHAPTER TWO
The 1993 Bills Comeback 11

CHAPTER THREE
A Masterful Performance 15

CHAPTER FOUR
Super Bowl Stunner 19

CHAPTER FIVE
A Game-Winning Streak 23

CHAPTER SIX
Peterson's Performance 27

Think About It 29
Glossary 30
Source Notes 31
To Learn More 32
Index 32

FAST FACTS

Game Rules

▶ A National Football League (NFL) game consists of four 15-minute quarters. Each team has 11 players on the field at one time.

▶ Teams can score a touchdown by getting into the end zone with the ball. A touchdown is worth six points. After a team makes a touchdown, it can either kick the football through the goalposts behind the end zone for one extra point or go for a two-point conversion.

▶ Teams can also score by kicking a field goal. A field goal is kicked through the goalposts and is worth three points.

The Super Bowl

▶ The top six teams in the National Football **Conference** and the American Football Conference make the playoffs each season. The teams then play three rounds of playoff games before the Super Bowl.

▶ The Super Bowl began after the 1966 season and features the winners of each conference.

Football is a physically demanding sport. ▶

CHAPTER ONE

THE PERFECT SEASON

Miami Dolphins head coach Don Shula sat on his players' shoulders as they **paraded** him around the stadium. After a long season, Shula and the Dolphins had finished their 1972 season strong and won the Super Bowl. That capped off the NFL's first—and still only—perfect season.

At the start of the season, Miami came out as an unstoppable force. The team kept winning every game. Miami faced challenges during its run for a perfect season. Quarterback Bob Griese got hurt in the fifth game of the season. He didn't return until the playoffs. Backup quarterback Earl Morrall came in and played well. He succeeded by making good passes and giving the ball to players such as star running back Mercury Morris. The Dolphins stayed undefeated through 14 regular season games. Then they won two playoff games.

◄ **Quarterback Bob Griese prepares to pass the football.**

▲ **Miami wide receiver Howard Twilley catches a pass during the Super Bowl.**

Their last stop was the Super Bowl in Los Angeles, California, against the Washington Redskins.

Miami's fans had something to cheer about early in the game. Griese returned from his injury and threw a touchdown pass that sailed over the heads of the Washington defense. The football fell into the arms of wide receiver Howard Twilley. He sprinted into the end zone, and the team took an early 7–0 lead.

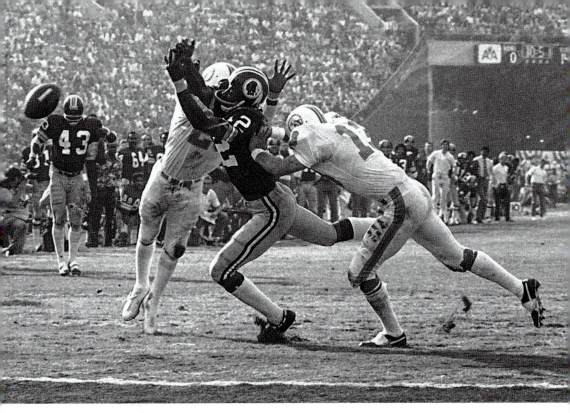

▲ **The Miami defense worked hard to stop Washington's offense.**

The Redskins were down 14–0 late in the game. Miami fans stood and watched with hopes that the Dolphins could stop Washington from scoring. The Redskins were close to the end zone. But a pass flew directly toward the defense. It was snatched up by Dolphins player Jake Scott. He ran up the field as the crowd roared with excitement.

Scott's **interception** helped secure the victory for Miami. The Dolphins had won the Super Bowl and completed the perfect season at 17–0. "It's not a record, it's an accomplishment," Morris said. "Records can be broken. Accomplishments can't."[1]

CHAPTER TWO

THE 1993 BILLS COMEBACK

All the Buffalo Bills could do was watch as the Houston Oilers scored once again to increase their lead to 35–3. Disappointed Bills players stood on the sidelines. The Oilers were red hot. The Bills needed to score 32 points in the second half just to tie the Oilers. And there was a lot on the line during this January 1993 first-round playoff game. The team that lost would be done for the season. The Bills would also have to accomplish this with their backup quarterback. Many people watching the game assumed that Buffalo's season was coming to an end.

But the Bills didn't give up. Instead, they got on their own hot streak. The team's comeback started with a few long passes from their quarterback, Frank Reich. His passes led to a touchdown, and the team also got an extra point, cutting Houston's lead to 35–10.

◀ **Bills players celebrate after scoring a touchdown against the Houston Oilers.**

▲ **Bills running back Thurman Thomas picks up some yards.**

Slowly, the game started to get closer. Buffalo had a pair of interceptions. And Reich was focused on scoring quickly. Midway through the third quarter, Reich threw a touchdown pass to star wide receiver Andre Reed. Then they connected for another one. The Bills went into the fourth trailing just 35–31.

When the Bills got the ball back again, Reich threw another pass right to Reed's hands. Reed sprinted away to score the touchdown. The Bills were now in the lead.

Houston fought back and tied the game to send it into overtime. The score was 38–38. The Bills got the ball and went to kick a field goal. The fans held their breath. The kick went up and through the goalposts, ending the game and giving Buffalo the win. It was the largest comeback in NFL history at the time. "Without question, it's the game of my life," Reich said.[2]

BEST POSTSEASON COMEBACKS IN THE NFL

TEAM	OPPONENT	DATE OF GAME	NUMBER OF POINTS BEHIND TO WIN
Buffalo Bills	Houston Oilers	January 3, 1993	32
Indianapolis Colts	Kansas City Chiefs	January 4, 2014	28
New England Patriots	Atlanta Falcons	February 5, 2017	25
San Francisco 49ers	New York Giants	January 5, 2003	24

CHAPTER THREE

A MASTERFUL PERFORMANCE

To people watching, San Francisco 49ers wide receiver Jerry Rice was just a red and gold flash as he ran down the middle of the field. There was no one around him. Rice kept running and patiently awaited the pass from his quarterback, Steve Young. The team was playing a *Monday Night Football* game against the Minnesota Vikings in 1995.

At the start of the game, Minnesota carefully covered Rice. Wherever he ran, Viking defenders followed him. They didn't want him to get the ball. The defense didn't bother Rice, though. San Francisco was moving the ball down the field well. But once the 49ers got close to the end zone, it was time for Rice to shine.

Young took the **snap** and looked at his receivers. He waited for Rice to get open. Rice put on a burst of speed and sprinted across the middle of the field, distancing himself from the defenders.

◄ **Jerry Rice picks up yardage against the Vikings.**

Rice saw the dark-brown ball spiraling toward him and caught it. Vikings players quickly ran in his direction, but Rice weaved past them. They fell down while trying to keep up with Rice. He easily walked into the end zone for the touchdown.

As the game went on, Rice began to utterly dominate the Vikings. Soon he was at it again. When he ran down the middle of the field, there was no one near him. Rice put his hand up, hoping Young would notice that he was open. Young saw him and delivered a throw right to Rice. He caught the ball and began sprinting toward the end zone. Minnesota defenders tried to catch him. By the time they did, Rice was in the end zone. It was another touchdown for Rice and the 49ers.

BRETT FAVRE'S MONDAY NIGHT MAGIC

One day before a big 2003 *Monday Night Football* game against the Oakland Raiders, Green Bay Packers quarterback Brett Favre got some awful news. His father had died. His father was a longtime football coach, and Favre decided that his dad would want him to play the next day. Favre did, and he had the game of a lifetime. He led the Packers to a 41–7 win while throwing for 399 yards and four touchdowns.

▲ **Steve Young threw his arms in the air after winning the game.**

This trend of Rice getting open continued. Whenever Young needed someone to throw to, Rice was there to make the catch. Rice scored his third touchdown after he made a Viking defender fall down with his quick **footwork**. It was a legendary performance as he had 14 catches for 289 yards and three touchdowns. It was his best game ever. San Francisco won 37–30.

CHAPTER FOUR

SUPER BOWL STUNNER

Running back Terrell Davis of the Denver Broncos was kneeling down on the field. He was hurt, but the pain wasn't coming from a knee or an arm injury. He was having a **migraine** headache during the Super Bowl in January 1998.

Davis had been key to the Broncos making it all the way to the Super Bowl. That season, he was on a rushing hot streak. He ran for 2,008 yards, making him the fourth player in league history to break 2,000 yards. But his migraine could've cost him a chance to play in the biggest game of his career.

Davis carefully stood up and slowly ran to the sidelines. Eventually, the migraine died down. Davis knew he could play again. He jogged back onto the field. He slipped his helmet on and was ready to go. His teammates were thrilled to see their star running back in the game once more.

◀ **Terrell Davis carries the ball during the Super Bowl.**

Davis began performing as if nothing had happened. Soon he was on a Super Bowl hot streak. He ran into defenders without a problem and even knocked some over and picked up extra yards. Davis's speed also made a big difference as he raced past Packers defenders. In the first quarter, he bulldozed his way into the end zone for a touchdown and celebrated in a **subtle** way. He gave a salute to the crowd and ran to the sidelines.

The two teams were nervous and excited when the final few minutes ticked down on the clock. The game was tied 24–24. Denver needed Davis to step up and continue his rushing hot streak. The Broncos were getting closer and closer to the end zone. When Denver was just outside the end zone, it was time for Davis to make a big play.

Broncos quarterback John Elway received the snap. He dropped back and handed the ball to Davis, who quickly ran past the defenders. There was an open path to the end zone. Davis saw it and sprinted forward quickly. He was inside the 5-yard line, and then he made it in for the touchdown. Denver had taken the lead on what proved to be the winning score, 31–24.

As the game ended, confetti streamed down onto the field. The Broncos won the Super Bowl. Davis finished with 157 yards and three touchdowns. He was also named Super Bowl MVP.

Davis raises the Super Bowl trophy in celebration. ▶

CHAPTER FIVE

A GAME-WINNING STREAK

New England Patriots kicker Adam Vinatieri was ready to kick a field goal. The yellow goalposts loomed in the distance. Before him stood the Carolina Panthers, dressed in their white uniforms streaked with blue. Everyone was waiting on Vinatieri. His kick could decide the winner of the Super Bowl in February 2004.

The Patriots had already won 14 games in a row before heading into the Super Bowl. If Vinatieri could make his 41-yard field goal to break the 29–29 tie, New England would pull ahead late in the game.

Outwardly, Vinatieri looked calm. This wasn't his first nerve-racking kick, and he was ready. The snap went directly to the holder. He put it down in the right spot for Vinatieri. Vinatieri took two steps forward and reached out to kick the ball.

◄ **Adam Vinatieri kicks a field goal during the Super Bowl.**

▲ **Quarterback Tom Brady signals to his teammates.**

It went soaring over the Carolina defense and through the goalposts. Vinatieri lifted his arms in victory as the stadium erupted in noise. New England went on to win the Super Bowl and continued its hot streak into the next season.

Eight months later, New England was in the middle of another strong season. The Patriots had already won a record 20 games in a row. Now, they were looking for a 21st **consecutive** win. They just had to beat the rival New York Jets.

New England was playing on a cold and dreary fall day in front of the hometown fans. The fans cheered wildly each time quarterback Tom Brady made a long pass down the field. The Patriots led 13–7 at halftime.

Whether the Patriots could win the game came down to their defense. New England needed to keep the Jets from moving forward one last time. The New York quarterback made a pass, but it was knocked away by a Patriot defender. Now, the Patriots could run down the clock and pick up their 21st win, with a final score of 13–7. Though the streak ended the next week with a loss to the Pittsburgh Steelers, New England had once again etched its name into the history books.

BRADY'S 2009 GAME VS. THE TENNESSEE TITANS

It took one quarter for Brady to make NFL history in 2009. The New England Patriots and Tennessee Titans faced off on a snowy October day in Foxborough, Massachusetts. Brady's hot streak started early in the second quarter. He launched a long pass to wide receiver Randy Moss, who extended his arms and beat the Titans defenders into the end zone. The perfect passes kept coming. Eventually, Brady ended up with five touchdown passes in less than 15 minutes. It was something the NFL had never seen before. "You never go into a game thinking it's going to be like this," said Patriots coach Bill Belichick. "It's just our day today."[3]

CHAPTER SIX

PETERSON'S PERFORMANCE

The game was just about over. The Minnesota Vikings led the San Diego Chargers 35–17 with a little more than one minute left in the fourth quarter. The Vikings had already all but secured a win over the Chargers in that 2007 game. Now, it was time for their starting running back to earn some glory. The fans in the stands stood on their feet. They were waiting for the moment when they would see history. Adrian Peterson was close to a record. Peterson had carried the ball well for Minnesota all day. His final carry wouldn't have any effect on the final score of the game. But it would have a major effect on Peterson's career as a running back.

San Diego knew Peterson was a main weapon on the Vikings' offense. On Peterson's first carry of the game, he sprinted to the open part of the field. Five Chargers moved quickly toward him.

◄ **Adrian Peterson races past a Chargers player.**

▲ **Peterson was a difficult player to tackle.**

The Vikings running back had nowhere to go and gained just 2 yards. But soon the yards began to add up.

The Chargers kept following Peterson around. But that didn't stop the Minnesota running back from making big plays. With the Vikings trailing 7–0 and just yards away from the end zone, Peterson got the ball. He kept his feet moving and pushed himself into the end zone for a touchdown.

Peterson's total yards kept piling up. In the third quarter, Peterson ran 64 yards for a touchdown. In the fourth, he had a 46-yard touchdown run. As the game went on, Peterson surpassed 200 yards. He needed 296 to break the single-game record. Eventually, whether he would break the record came down to the final carry. Peterson needed only three more yards.

The snap went to the Vikings quarterback. He handed the ball to Peterson. He ran into a group of players from both teams. Keeping his feet moving, Peterson managed to pick up those 3 yards. He hit 296 yards to break the previous record of 295. The crowd knew it and gave a resounding cheer. They had witnessed a record-breaking day from their star running back.

THINK ABOUT IT

- Both teams and individual players can accomplish different milestones. Which type of milestone do you think is most impressive? Explain your answer.
- Football is one of the most popular sports in the United States. Why do you think so many people like to watch football?
- Do you think winning a game comes down to teamwork, the skills of individual players, or both? Explain your answer.

GLOSSARY

conference (KAHN-fur-uhns): A conference is a group of teams. The NFL has the National Football Conference and the American Football Conference.

consecutive (kuhn-SEK-yuh-tiv): Consecutive means it happened in a row. The Patriots had 21 consecutive wins.

footwork (FUT-wurk): Footwork is the way someone moves their feet. The wide receiver got around the defense by using good footwork.

interception (in-tur-SEP-shun): An interception is when the defense catches a pass from the quarterback. An interception allowed the defense to score points.

migraine (MY-grayn): A migraine is a bad headache that can cause vomiting or other pain. A migraine forced Davis to leave the game for a while.

paraded (puh-RAYD-ed): To be paraded is to go around in a proud fashion. The head coach was paraded around the field after the team won.

snap (SNAP): A snap occurs when the center hands the ball to the quarterback to start the play. The quarterback took the snap and threw the ball.

subtle (SUHT-uhl): To be subtle is to have done a little thing that can be hard to notice. The coach made a subtle change to his appearance by moving his pencil from his left ear to his right ear.

SOURCE NOTES

1. David Whitley. "For 1972 Miami Dolphins, Pride Is in the Accomplishment, Not the Record." *Sporting News.* Sporting News Media, 3 Dec. 2012. Web. 21 Jan. 2019.

2. Vic Carucci. "Bills—Greatest Comeback." *Pro Football Hall of Fame.* Pro Football Hall of Fame, 1 Jan. 2005. Web. 21 Jan. 2019.

3. "Brady Throws Six TD Passes as Patriots Ice Winless Titans." *ESPN.* ESPN Internet Ventures, 19 Oct. 2009. Web. 21 Jan. 2019.

TO LEARN MORE

BOOKS

Anastasio, Dina. *What Is the Super Bowl?* New York, NY: Grosset & Dunlap, 2015.

Bryant, Howard. *Legends: The Best Players, Games, and Teams in Football.* New York, NY: Philomel Books, 2015.

Sports Illustrated Kids. *The Greatest Football Teams of All Time.* New York, NY: Time Inc. Books, 2018.

WEBSITES

Visit our website for links about the NFL: **childsworld.com/links**

Note to Parents, Teachers, and Librarians: We routinely verify our Web links to make sure they are safe and active sites. So encourage your readers to check them out!

INDEX

Brady, Tom, 24–25
Buffalo Bills, 11–13

Davis, Terrell, 19–20
Denver Broncos, 19–20

Favre, Brett, 16

Griese, Bob, 7–8

interception, 12

Miami Dolphins, 7–9
Minnesota Vikings, 15–17, 27–29

New England Patriots, 23–25

Peterson, Adrian, 27–29

Reich, Frank, 11–13
Rice, Jerry, 15–17

San Francisco 49ers, 15–17
Super Bowl, 4, 7–9, 19–20, 23–24